DIGGING UP DINOSAURS

For Hiroshi and Miyoko

This Is a Let's-Read-and-Find-Out Book™

DIGGING UP DINOSAURS

by ALIKI

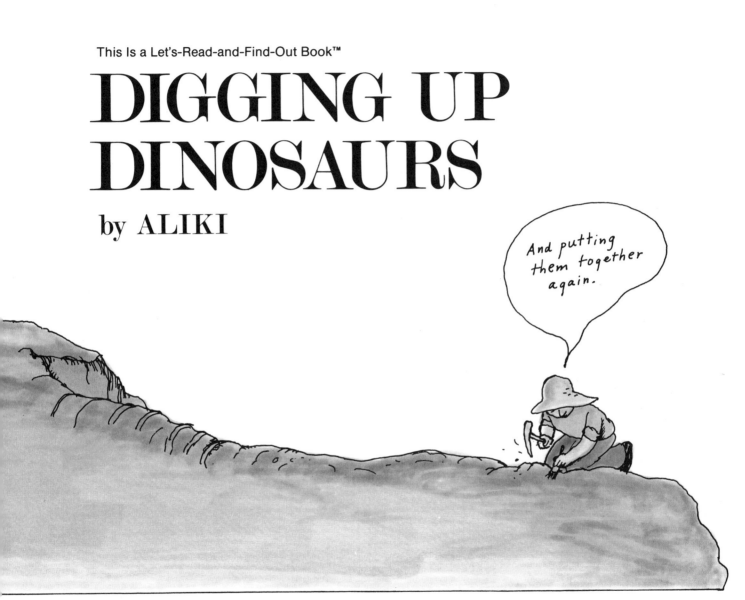

And putting them together again.

A Harper Trophy Book
Harper & Row, Publishers

The *Let's-Read-and-Find-Out Book*™ series was originated by Dr. Franklyn M. Branley, Astronomer Emeritus and former Chairman of The American Museum-Hayden Planetarium, and was formerly co-edited by him and Dr. Roma Gans, Professor Emeritus of Childhood Education, Teachers College, Columbia University. Text and illustrations for each of the more than 100 books in the series are checked for accuracy by an expert in the relevant field. The titles available in paperback are listed below. Look for them at your local bookstore or library.

Other Recent Let's-Read-and-Find-Out Books™ You Will Enjoy

Digging Up Dinosaurs.
Copyright © 1981 by Aliki Brandenberg
All rights reserved. Printed in the United States of America.
No part of this book may be used or reproduced
in any manner whatsoever without written permission
except in the case of brief quotations embodied in
critical articles and reviews. For information address
Thomas Y. Crowell Junior Books, 10 East 53rd Street,
New York, N.Y. 10022. Published simultaneously in
Canada by Fitzhenry & Whiteside Limited, Toronto.
Published in hardcover by
Thomas Y. Crowell, New York.

Library of Congress Cataloging in Publication Data
Aliki.
  Digging up dinosaurs.

  (Let's-Read-and-Find-Out Science Book)
  Summary: Briefly introduces various types of dino-
saurs whose skeletons and reconstructions are seen in mu-
seums and explains how scientists uncover, preserve, and
study fossilized dinosaur bones.
  1. Dinosaurs—Juvenile literature.   2. Paleontology—
Collectors and collecting—Juvenile literature. [1. Dinosaurs.
2. Fossils] I. Title.
QE862.D5A34   567.9'1   80-2250
ISBN 0-690-04098-9
ISBN 0-690-04099-7 (lib. bdg.)
ISBN 0-06-445016-3 (pbk.)

DIGGING UP DINOSAURS

Have you ever seen dinosaur skeletons
  in a museum?
I have.
I visit them all the time.
I went again yesterday.

I saw APATOSAURUS.

I saw CORYTHOSAURUS.

I saw IGUANODON and TRICERATOPS.
I like to say their names.

STEGOSAURUS was just where I had left it.
And TYRANNOSAURUS REX looked as fierce
   as ever.
TYRANNOSAURUS used to scare me.
I still can't believe how big it is.
Just its head is almost twice my size.

I'm not afraid of dinosaurs anymore.
Sometimes I call them "you bag of bones"
   under my breath.
I can spend hours looking at them.
I used to wonder where they came from
   and how they got into the museum.
But now I know.

I'm scared!

Here he is!

Hello, up there.

STEGOSAURUS
(PLATED DINOSAUR)
PLANT-EATER

4

The king.

TYRANNOSAURUS REX
MEAT-EATER

5

Dinosaurs lived millions of years ago.
A few of them were as small as birds,
but most were enormous.

ORNITHOMIMUS

TYRANNOSAURUS

Some dinosaurs ate plants.
Some dinosaurs ate the meat of other dinosaurs,
and some may even have eaten the eggs
    of other dinosaurs.

Dinosaurs lived everywhere.
They lived on every continent in the world.

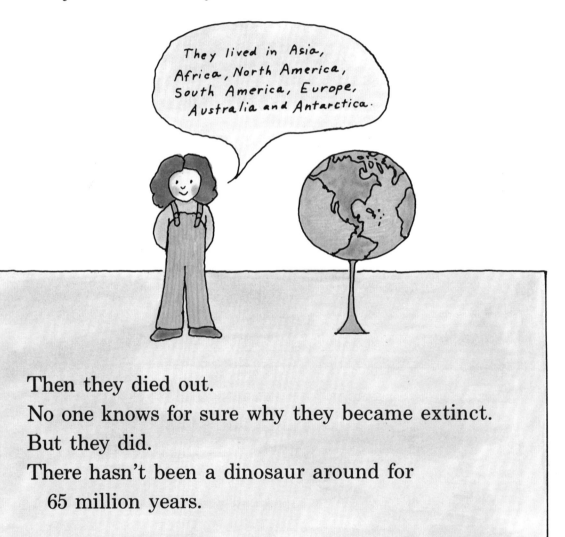

They lived in Asia, Africa, North America, South America, Europe, Australia and Antarctica.

Then they died out.
No one knows for sure why they became extinct.
But they did.
There hasn't been a dinosaur around for
65 million years.

Until about 200 years ago, no one knew
  anything about dinosaurs.
Then people began finding things in rock.
They found large footprints.
They found huge, mysterious bones
  and strange teeth.
People were finding fossils.

Fossils are a kind of diary of the past.
They are the remains of plants and animals
    that died long ago.
Instead of rotting or crumbling away, the remains
    were preserved, and slowly turned to stone.

① 80 million years ago

Dinosaur dies and sinks into river.

② Its flesh rots.
Its skeleton is covered by sand.

③ In time, the sand and skeleton turn to stone.

④ Dinosaur is hidden for millions of years.

⑤ The earth changes.
Some of the stone breaks away.

⑥ 200 years ago

Part of dinosaur shows.

Fossils tell about life on earth long ago. Everything we know about dinosaurs comes from studying fossils.

Fossil hunters found more and more big bones
  in different parts of the world.
Scientists studied the fossils.
They said the bones and teeth and footprints
  all belonged to a group of giant reptiles
  that lived on earth for millions of years.
The giants were named DINOSAURIA,
  or TERRIBLE LIZARD.

1822
Mary Ann Mantell found
the first dinosaur fossils
in England.
  She discovered some
giant fossil teeth.

1825
Her husband, Gideon Mantell,
named the animal
IGUANODON, or IGUANA-
TOOTH.
Nine years later he
found an IGUANODON
skeleton.

1841
Richard Owen named
the giant reptiles
DINOSAURIA.

What finds these were!
People crowded into museums to see them.
But the dinosaur bones didn't just get up
and walk there.
They had to be dug out of the ground,
slowly and patiently.

13

Even today, digging up dinosaurs is not an easy job.
A team of experts must work together.

PALEONTOLOGIST
A scientist who
studies ancient
plants and animals.

GEOLOGIST
A scientist who
knows the age of
rocks and fossils.

DRAFTSMAN
Who draws pictures
of the fossils.

WORKERS
Who dig the fossil out of the rock.

PHOTOGRAPHER
Who takes pictures of the find.

SPECIALISTS
Who prepare the fossil for the museum.

15

This is how fossil hunters work.
First, they have to find a dinosaur.
They search along riverbanks and in quarries.
They climb up high cliffs, and down
into steep canyons.

Dinosaurs have been found in quarries, where rock is cut for use in buildings and roads.

With luck, someone spots a fossil bone
poking through the rock.
The site is covered with a tent,
and the work begins.

Sometimes the fossil is buried so deep, the rock
 around it has to be drilled or blasted.
Tons of rubble are carted away.
Scientists chip at the rock close to the fossil.
They brush away the grit.
They have to be very careful.

As soon as a bone is uncovered,
  it is brushed with shellac.
The shellac helps hold the bone together,
  so it won't crumble.
Then the bone is numbered.

Sometimes a skeleton has to be cut apart
  so that it can be moved.
The draftsman draws each bone in its
  exact position, and the photographer
  takes pictures.
That way, there can be no mix-up later,
  when someone tries to put the skeleton
  together.

When the bones are ready to be moved,
they are carefully wrapped.
Small bones are wrapped in tissue paper,
and put into boxes or sacks.

Large bones are left half-buried in rock.
They will be dug out later, in the museum.
These fossils are covered with a plaster cast,
    just as a broken leg is.

First, the parts of the fossil that show are covered with wet tissue paper, and then with strips of burlap dipped in wet plaster. Then the whole piece is wrapped in the same way. When the plaster dries, it becomes very hard. The tissue paper covering makes the cast easier to remove later.

Each bone is then packed in straw, put in crates,
and taken to the museum.

At the museum, scientists unwrap the fossil.
They finish digging it out of the rock.
They study the bones.

Scientists dig out the fossil in many different ways. They use a hammer and chisel, fine needles, power tools like a dentist's drill, special sand-blasting machines, or even chemicals that dissolve the rock but do not harm the fossil.

They compare the bones to other dinosaur bones.
They compare them to the bones of other animals.
They try to figure out what size and shape
   the dinosaur was.
They try to find out how the dinosaur stood
   and walked, and what it ate.

IGUANODON

First discovered and named by
DR. GIDEON MANTELL in England, 1825

AGE: 115 MILLION YEARS OLD
PERIOD: LOWER CRETACEOUS
LENGTH: 9 METERS (30 FEET)
WEIGHT: 5,000 POUNDS
TYPE: ORNITHISCHIAN (BIRD HIP)
         HERBIVOROUS (PLANT-EATER)
   DESCENDED FROM DINOSAUR CAMPTOSAURUS.

This information has been gathered by studying many IGUANODON finds from all over the world.

Bird hip.

Rough skin.
Exact color unknown.

Spiked thumbs used for digging and protection.

Usually walked on two legs.
Hoof-like bones show it sometimes walked on its front limbs.

Tail used for balancing.

Horny beak used to tear up plants.

Thousands of flat teeth used to grind food. When teeth wore out, they fell out and others grew in.

Here is its hip bone.

	TODAY	0
CENOZOIC	QUATERNARY	
	TERTIARY	
	UPPER CRETACEOUS	65
	LOWER CRETACEOUS	
MESOZOIC		136
	UPPER JURASSIC	
	LOWER JURASSIC	193
	UPPER TRIASSIC	
	LOWER TRIASSIC	225
	PERMIAN	
	CARBONIFEROUS	280
PALEOZOIC	DEVONIAN	345
	SILURIAN	395
	ORDOVICIAN	435
	CAMBRIAN	500
		570
PRE-CAMBRIAN		
	AGE OF EARTH	4600

MILLIONS OF YEARS
AGE OF DINOSAURS

27

If there are enough bones, scientists are able
  to build a complete skeleton.
A frame is made in the shape of the dinosaur
  to support the bones.
The bones are wired together, one by one.
They are held in place with pieces of metal.
If any bones are missing, plastic or fiberglass ones
  are made to replace them.
You can hardly tell the new bones from the old.

After many months the work is complete.
The dinosaur skeleton looks just as it once did.

29

Until recently, only a few museums had dinosaurs.
Then scientists learned to make copies of the skeletons.
The copy is hard to make.
It takes a long time.
The original skeleton has to be taken completely
   apart, bone by bone.
A mold is made for each bone.

The new pieces are made of fiberglass.
A fiberglass dinosaur is just as scary as
   the original, but much stronger and lighter.

The original bone is covered with rubber latex and an outer coating of fiberglass to hold the rubber stiff. This is peeled off the bone to form the mold. The inside is brushed with resin and filled with fiberglass. Many dinosaurs can be made from the same molds.

Now museums all over the world have dinosaur skeletons.
And many people can spend hours looking
at them, the way I do.

See you in the museum sometime!

ABOUT THE AUTHOR—ILLUSTRATOR

Aliki has been fascinated by dinosaurs and their world ever since she was introduced to them by her two young children. Now that her children are grown, she wanted to write the book she wished she had had then to answer their questions—and hers. The author of many other popular books in the Let's-Read-and-Find-Out series, including *Wild and Woolly Mammoths, Fossils Tell of Long Ago,* and *My Visit to the Dinosaurs,* her *Corn Is Maize* was named First Prize Book for 1976 by the New York Academy of Sciences.

Long-time residents of New York City, Aliki and her husband, Franz, also a children's book author, now live with their children, Jason and Alexa, in London.